FELLING

FELLING

KELAN NEE

WINNER 2023 VASSAR MILLER PRIZE IN POETRY

University of North Texas Press
Denton, Texas

Printed in the United States of America.

10 9 8 7 6 5 4 3 2 1

Permissions:
University of North Texas Press
1155 Union Circle #311336
Denton, TX 76203-5017

The paper used in this book meets the minimum requirements of the American National Standard for Permanence of Paper for Printed Library Materials, z39.48.1984. Binding materials have been chosen for durability.

Library of Congress Cataloging-in-Publication Data

Names: Nee, Kelan, 1995- author.
Title: Felling / Kelan Nee.
Other titles: Vassar Miller prize in poetry series ; no. 31.
Description: Denton, Texas : University of North Texas, [2024] | Series:
    Number 31 in the Vassar Miller prize in poetry series | "Winner 2023
    Vassar Miller Prize in Poetry."
Identifiers: LCCN 2024009198 (print) | LCCN 2024009199 (ebook) |
    ISBN 9781574419313 (paperback) | ISBN 9781574419405 (ebook)
Subjects: LCSH: Distress (Psychology)--Poetry. | Emotional conditioning--Poetry. |
    BISAC: POETRY / American / General | LCGFT: Poetry.
Classification: LCC PS3614.E268 F45 2024 (print) | LCC PS3614.E268
    (ebook) | DDC 811/.6--dc23/eng/20240229
LC record available at https://lccn.loc.gov/2024009198
LC ebook record available at https://lccn.loc.gov/2024009199

Felling is Number 31 in the Vassar Miller Poetry Prize Series

Cover image, "Perfume" by artist Ivan Ríos-Fetchko, oil and wax on paper over panel in steel frame, 30.5 x 44.5 x 2 inches, 2022, from a private collection.

The electronic edition of this book was made possible by the support of the Vick Family Foundation.

For my father,
who took some light with him
when he left the world

CONTENTS

•

SPARKS IN THE SUN

My father's hands were roped with scars
from burns at work. He had trouble
bending his fingers. The ache.
I watched him debone a perch

at sundown, run his ragged hands
over the thin thing, the spine curling
like rosemary from his grip
and onto the ground. My neighbor

asked for a jump, clapped the copper jaws
to make sparks in the sun. Then
he offered me meth for my car.
The woman I'm seeing has hands nearly

as big as mine. We share each other's shoes.
She says I'll come to hate her
if I stay long enough. I can't
make sense of anything, but

I disagree. I cut my hand this week
on the bramble spines that grow thick
in the forest. I didn't notice till I looked
and saw blood all over the door.

The light today shows all the moving pieces.
I think I can see them when I step out
and into the sun. My whole body hurts:

an unholy choir. My dad is gone: his hands
did it to him. I try to keep busy. I hold
her hands. I clean the blood off the door.

RUBY THROAT

Tonight, I can see you lifting the small body
of a bird up from the beach. You were awed
by their flight across the gulf, and their collapse.
You said it was not failure. No. A bird can't
help itself. That I'm like that, but you wouldn't say
how. Little wings that can't quit. The moon
has got some light in it. I can see it from my table.
Pale and smooth—the snow quenched with it.
I'm alone, bundles of dead flowers for dry company.
There'd been a plume of dust, heat coming up,
and us, passing a cigarette across daybreak. You
looked me in the eye, small red blaze peeking
from between your fingers. You shivered,
unblinking, and held it out, toward me.

FELLING

The girl in Dickey Bub working the register looked at me
like I was food. She couldn't have been older than fifteen.
She watched me leave and drive away. I was going to be alone.
Among the trees which were easy with me. I saw a boy with a gun
as big as his body, stood butt-end up; a spotted dog, curled,
sleeping on top of a truck; a woman who sold me two dozen eggs
from inside of her house; a beagle, brain bashed, tossed
on the side of the road like salt. Everything made me sad.
I was used to this kind of driving sadness, that made me believe
that being alive was unbearable, and the only thing worth doing.
I ran a saw for two days, dropped what must've been thirty trees.
Post oak. Shortleaf pine. Black oak. Catalpa. Post oak. Post oak.
My body felt useful again and my mind quiet. In the morning,
I ate eggs, and kicked my feet into boots. At night, I ate eggs,
and looked up. I didn't feel bad, felling trees though they had done
nothing to deserve falling. In the city, I had someone waiting for me.
There I had forgotten color and silence, and I had only been a mind
made of words and yet, with her, my body had roots. I thought of her,
endlessly. I ate sixteen eggs in two days. I breathed heavier
than I should have. I sat in the woods when I couldn't lift my arms.
Years before, in the forest in Maine, I lived alone. I would fill a bucket
with water from a spring and pour it over myself. My bare body
like a field. Once, I was watched. Hikers, making their way off trail.
I turned to grab my towel from a branch. They smiled and said hello.
I said it back. Sitting against a stump this week, I thought of them,
my chest heaving, my body a ziggurat of salt. In the morning, I drove
to Iron County. The man in the hardware store, camo-clad and hulking,
looked at me like a deer. I needed something to kill rats, whose tails
had been thrumming through the night. He showed me the poison,
a bar of dust and glue. Unwrapped it, held it up to his mouth. Winked.
I didn't go back to the cabin. I didn't want to be useful. I didn't want
the trees. I drove fast, back to her, who made me breathless, afraid.
Who made me believe I was good, and my body could be enjoyed.

WORTH

I used to run joists for support and lay
stringers for stairs. On roofs I went
unharnessed. Now I am 26.
I ice my back and my wrists. Rest
my concussed brain. I spend all day walking
in the park, and still get paid. Note
how gently the breeze trembles the cypress.
How similar it is to the thin hair that shimmers
on my lover's wrist. I used to be useful,
I'm sure. I think I may be sick. I think
I can only be sad. Every person I have loved
has told me that they have wanted to die.
I told my mother. I suppose I could've kept
it to myself. I don't know if this is useful
to say. The playground is empty.
Everyone is at work. The aluminum
is hot to the touch, built in primary colors.

EARLY IN LOVE

We were young and lean with lanklust,
yearning for long limbs and sweat, weary
of reality and its seriousness that summer.
We lived in the back of my car. You drove

when I couldn't, from the drinking, or fatigue
that lined the roads. We wanted each other
like hands want handles, and often wrapped
our bodies around the other's frame anywhere

that we could find. Once, in the Walmart
parking lot, we were caught. Only a T-shirt
hanging over the window for privacy. A man
with a tattoo that read *Chevrolet* on his arm

caught my collar while I fumbled for the keys.
You were lying in the back seat, folded down,
while he tore the fabric around me. You told me
later that night that you loved me. I told you

that love was only a word to me. That I carried it
in my mouth the way an owl mangles a mouse
until it can swallow it whole before sleep.
I was wrong to say it. You told me

I only loved pain. You said, I wish you would push
your tongue against me like a sore in your mouth.

HIS BODY CUT THROUGH
THE WORLD LIKE A COLD WIND

The temperature pushes us inside. Sometimes
I think remembering is just giving the limbs
back to a body you once held in your arms.
Giving it life, letting it do whatever it wants with you.
I make myself forget.
In the house we are destroying, each room is asking
to be taken apart. The crowbar pries the walls away
from the floors and reveals an object. Behind the drywall,
a Barbie doll, hair trimmed. Beneath the floorboards,
a diary wrapped in string. Our own small homes
are falling apart. We destroy these houses for people.
For money. They tell us they couldn't bear to keep living
inside. You, who knew what it meant to self-destruct,
would understand. Fire burns down the forest: fuel.
They say suicide can be inherited, a seed that feeds
on a brain. It grows like a tree until the dirt
from which it came can't handle its new weight.
Outside the wind blows.
A feeling like falling, weightless. A feeling I find myself
surprised at standing in front of a house I'll never live in.
It's my job to give the people who pay a place to live.
I have nowhere besides my truck, a small room, the drugs
I put in my body and the smoke in my lungs.
We tell each other we want to live in places that look beautiful.
Places where birds sing. It happens every year. It's happening.
It is October again, so the birds can be shot from the sky.
We can clip their wings with bullets for a fee.
I am always surprised at how warm it is inside a body.
The air bites at my hands and the carcass like a blanket.
I pull the liver and put it in a bag. Throw the heart to the dog.
Another angel shot out of the sky, blood red against
a world fading in fall. So much is beginning to die.
I stay inside mostly, feeling

9

allowed by the clouds. Bear my head to the world to smoke a
cigarette or buy a meal. I like the silence of winter coming.
A hush has forced the world toward whisper.
It is easier, that quiet music, sung like stories we tell
ourselves to keep on going. At night sometimes, I put
my face out into the air, for no reason other than to see
the breath that rises from my mouth.
Life that contains proof of living. Tonight, I can see it.
The world has been beautiful today. It will be beautiful
tomorrow too. It is my father who creeps around the rooms
of my mind after I thought I had emptied them. I haven't told
the men at work how he died. We haven't said aloud
that all of them are old enough to have me as a son.
It is dangerous work that we do. The spinning metal,
the biting screws. We don't talk about the things that scare us.
The farmer and I, took the tails from the lambs
when they were young. As if they would forget having them.
It's easy, we told ourselves, painless even.
The farmer held one down,
a week or two after being pushed out into hay bales and I
stretched a rubber band over the small shaft at its rear.
When we cut their throats later, we counted the tails.
Pinned them somewhere. Counted the bodies. Compared.
See how many we'd lost. The ones taken or died without us
using our hands. Every splintered thing about me, to the world,
is just another breaking. Nowhere near the number of boards
I have broken. We like to call the frame of a house a skeleton.
Say things like *it's an old house, but it's got good bones.*
My job is to build a body, dress it up, and invite people in.
To beat it with a hammer, and cut it with a saw.
All these tools we've used on wood could be used on our bodies.
The houses' bones no different from our own. No one on the job
forgets. The truth is that I could only hurt myself. At work,
I do everything not to. My hands busy and moving. My mind
forgetting for a day. In the mirror my face becomes his.
He looks me in the eyes every morning. He was a chef, and knew
the importance of hands. Their power. He comes to me in dreams,

at work, in thin strips of tomatoes in the kitchen. I wonder
if his hands were shaking when he did it. If he was drunk
enough to forget he was my father. Anyway, his lack became
his being. Each missing thing, a reminder. He reminds me
to use my hands every day and I remind myself to use them well.
He reminds me that every dying thing belongs to someone.
The birds and sheep, the cows whose life my hands have spilled
into the dirt. All things gone are also him. All things living
only things waiting to be gone. I try to build things that cannot die,
but even they sink. The cow I killed never closed its eyes.
I mean even after it was empty of blood, organs and meat,
its giant head kept looking at me. We cut it off with a saw.
Turned its skin to leather. The farmer's friend wears it around now.
We threw the head away. Like it was trash. Like it didn't
contain a tongue. I'm still angry about that. Not that it died.
That I see the head. A head I held in my hands, brushing
the back below it, when it was living. The truth is, the head
doesn't only haunt. It also helps. I spend time trying to keep
the dead away, but every day, the dead make themselves
alive. They are here. Bodies surround me at work.
The men who I hardly talk to. They care for me,
silent. When it finally happened, I was surprised.
My hand got clipped by the saw. My finger burst into blood
and for a moment I forgot everything.
Pain eliminates, then illuminates.
I was bleeding and all the men ran
to me, one wrapped his shirt around my hand.
I was a child again, skinned knee and my father washing it.
The world comes rushing back.

INHERITANCE

I was eleven. My father called. My cousin was dead. 18.
My cousin. Hooked on hope, hit a cop across the face
with a 2x4, high, in the middle of Lowe's. He saw a chance
and took it. Hanged himself with his bedsheets in the criminal
hospital. When I started crying, my dad told me to stop.
When I asked questions, he answered them.
He never lied to me.

He was coming home, for the wake and funeral, to wrap
his sister in his arms. He was sober then and thought
he was sober for good. It was winter in Massachusetts, and so,
like every other place with snow on the ground, small stars
and the thin moon hanging above, it never quite got dark.
I remember his voice. What he said before he hung up. *Listen.*
Your mother and me would never do anything like this.
You hear me?

I remember my father's freckled hands on my shoulders
as men lowered my cousin into a hole. That a machine had to do
the digging, the dirt too hard for a shovel. And my father's tie.
The colors, muted and washed. The one he gave me. It was too big
for me then, but fit when I wore it to his funeral five years later.
He had put it around my neck, showed me how to make a knot
and slip it up. So that it was tight, but not too tight,
against my throat.

A FRIEND

He was the first man I ever loved,
though we were boys then.
Walking the park at night softly

telling each other that we were
alive and able to hold one
another. That year his DUI nearly

killed him, though he still won't
admit it. Then, at my house
he sat silently while I mourned

my father and his will to live.
A mourning of realization, blue
and warm, that I didn't love my dad

so entirely until he was dead,
that I should love someone living.
My friend didn't say a word. Silent

when cigarette burns turned up
on my arms and the backs of my hands.
He knew what it meant to hurt himself

in a way that only he could. Pain
that made meaning of pain. I saw the holes
he put in his walls, the paint he inhaled,

the flattened Volvo, rolled easy.
I was silent too. A body to be beside.
We were one for a while. Look at us then

drinking, smoke pouring from our mouths.
Those nights so thick with us
and our longing. The grass crawling

over our toes like fog. Both happy
to have a body beside us,
nearly, but never, gone.

GRAFFITI

                 Young, we would wait
for snowbanks to gather, and climb them
with cans of paint in our hands. My friend
wrote *DUK* fifteen feet above the ground.
I was never any good at it. It meant a lot
to the boys I loved to be there.
We didn't know what to do with ourselves
so, we walked. Sometimes hey-mistered
our ways into a couple of beers. Loose
cigarettes. On a dark path once, a swaying
man gave us a bottle of something with
formaldehyde mixed in. We let the shadows
do their work. We'd stuff steaks and cuts
of pork into our waistbands. Tell people
doing their jobs to fuck themselves. Go home
to houses with mothers in them. Mothers
who loved us, and who we resented for that.
For now, I don't feel like dying anymore
and I'm learning to trust it. *DUK* is still
there, fading and arched. All of my friends
are still alive somehow. Though of course
that can't last. We behave better now.
And nearly every day I think of coming across
a dying bird. Twitching thing. My friends
and I watched it. Surely someone had a stick.
When one of us stomped hard on its head
all of us screamed. The world was breathtaking
when we all wanted to disappear. We ran
screaming, laughing, looking back, looking
ahead, looking at each other. Dodging cars,
horns laid, as they drove across the street.
When we came too close, our thin fingers
left streaks in the dust that coated the paint.

SEVENTEEN

In the mow field I would ride a tractor.
First hay, second hay, if we were lucky a third.
The engine would turn over, choke and roar.
Reach its monotone, its growl and hum.

Circles. I had to ride them tight. I made
sure to hit each slender stalk of grass. Bruce,
the farmer, lay inside, in the dark, not drinking,
listening to music, doing everything not to lose.

His wife, Chris, made cheese. I was only a year
into my grief. It was young and demanding.
It hung on to my legs and hid from strangers.
On the tractor, I would cut the wheel hard

at field ends. I would steer with my knees
at straightaways. Look over and back
near the edges of the grass. There was a river,
immense, the biggest in New England, that

chortled through the land beside me. I could
see it from my tower of a seat on the old Ford.
The last time Bruce drank, there was a flood.
All of their pumpkins gone and riding the river

down to Massachusetts. He downed a bottle,
and picked up a gun. Went to the green shore
and shot everything he could. So many crops,
cows, chairs, whole sides of barns raged by.

That had been more than twenty years before
and by the time we met he was quiet. We were
flush with pumpkins, meat, milk.
Every time I mowed I would set off silent.

Then I would sing. Start crying. Over the sound
of the engine, I couldn't even hear myself.
I would get louder. I would dig in. Sometimes,
I felt like screaming. Sometimes, I screamed.

STILLBORN

She broke her chain, charged after me
while I ran her baby to the birthing pen.

I'd found it in the gutter, with his mother's manure and urine
fresh, hardly born, and her hollering to let him walk,

only stopping to lick him once I'd let him go, dove out of the way.
We watched from the wooden fencing of the pen

and when the dead one came, it slipped out, yellow,
half formed, as if pickled, too small to live.

She turned for a moment to look at it, her dead child,
a bull calf, and the barn floated, swayed while she sniffed.

I had never known a cow could howl until she pitched her head,
screamed at the ceiling, begging it to come down.

She turned her tongue to the living son,
lurching toward me each time I looked at him.

I walked in later and lifted the stillborn into a shoebox,
her only snorting at me from the corner.

I buried it in the pumpkin field under a baby shower sky
letting her alone with him that night since the dead had died,

and she chose instead to lick the living. I took enough painkillers,
two mornings later as the sun rose, that I didn't feel

her horns in my side, the cracking of ribs, as I pulled her calf
out of the pen, chained him to a wall, and shoved his face

into bowls of milk till he learned to drink from a pail,
until he started running to me, instead of his mother.

CLOSE ENOUGH NOT TO HURT

We keep quiet at work, letting the mouths of our saws
whir and spin. Like us, their teeth can ruin, separate.
A raised voice here is a fearful one.

Once I saw Ben shoot a nail through his palm,
and into a pine joist. His hand sucked
the noise out of the air. There was no thud or thunk

that comes with metal meeting wood. Stigmata-ed,
he looked nothing like Christ. He looked scared, awake.
Honest. He whimpered, looking across the dust and room,

into my eyes. He was on a ladder, and so pinned,
with his heels in the air, only his toes and the nail holding him up.
I pulled it from the wood, his nail and hand. I felt

his breath on my neck. Outside we smoked,
before he drove himself to the ER. In that smokeshame
and cold, steam rose. Neither of us mentioned

our bodies were haunted. By the dead, sure, but more
than the dead. All of the things that had been done
to our bodies and all of the things we knew

we could do to them. Inside, the shriek of a saw
and something once living being shoved into its mouth.

KILL SWITCH

Someone broke into my car
last night and took nothing.
I walked out in the morning
to find open doors and paper
all over the front seats.

They'd pulled the registration
from the glove. My passport.
Left the coins in the cup holders.
My father had an Altima
that wouldn't lock. He taught me

never to leave anything inside—
every night someone would break in.
Every day those silver doors
blown open and the napkins
wind-drawn across the pavement

and grass. It scared me to see
how comfortable my father was
knowing nothing belonged to him.
He taught me: He drove the car
to an empty house one night,

and made himself into a breathless
body. An absence. I put the paper
back where it belonged and sat
where a stranger had been.

SUPPER POEM

My father comes to me in dreams, always dead and happy
to see me. We're quiet together, standing at cutting boards
side by side. It's been a decade since he died.

I would stay with him when I was young and he played sober
well enough to fool my mom. He'd pick me up on days off
from the restaurant where he worked as a line cook

and snuck drinks from behind the bar. Before he got fired, and sober
for the next to last time, he broke in, drank as much as his body could bear.
They found him on the floor, sweat glistening on his face.

Back then, he rarely cooked for me. Sometimes for supper, he pulled a bar
of chocolate from his coat, Hershey's Special Dark, and broke half
off for him and half for me. He'd put both squares between slices

of white bread, and put on a Bruce Springsteen record. We took bites,
his big and mine small. We'd drink cream soda. He used to take me
up in his arms like I was made of cotton and cloth. Hold me so close

to his chest that I could feel his breath on my hair. He told me he loved me.
He did. He said that he was scared something would take me away.
An eagle or a hawk. That it would kill him if anything ever hurt me.

He would tuck me in. I'd hear the suck of a cork being pulled from a bottle,
the tap of Newports against his palm. The door, open and shut.

SLOW CREAKING

There is a perfect moment when you're building a room.
Dust glinting off the air and hot from breath and tools,
you could glance from one particular angle and see
that the studs have all fallen in line. It's as if there is one
stud, one pillar of thin wood that holds the entire space up
on its own. We used to say how odd it was, in our way,
between beers and music, screech and grunt,
that a room seemed so much smaller stud-stripped and open.
It was as if the idea of a room made a room minute. Then
the drywall gets fastened, painted, the baseboard and molding
coped together. It feels huge, at least the size of a room.
It must be the eye's impulse to understand. Maybe it doesn't
mean much, to notice. But that moment of looking and seeing—
It's like driving and seeing rows off crops, wherever
rows of crops are grown. Speed gives you a glimpse
of order. Or accident. Then a return to what else there is.
My father is on my mind again, though he is not often far from it.
I wonder if he would know what I mean. If he saw the world in
moments. If he had the peace not to attempt sense of them. I doubt it.
I've seen people the way I've seen a room, from one angle
for one second. I shouldn't do that. I worked once with a man,
Brent, on an irrigation team. He told me it kept him up
at night, thinking about the sprinklers. Most days we would
use a radio to call in to the control system. In the half-day morning
small pillars would rise, and water would kick on. That arc was his
moment. Neither of us knew then that he was my father
the way that every man I've known has been my father. I don't
know if that's so true anymore. I saw Brent cry once, when
Tom Petty died. We took the day off and drank bloody mary's
in the afternoon. I saw the moment of perfection with his lips
red, above slumped shoulders, and *American Girl* seeping out.
I never saw my dad cry, though I know he did.
I've made the mistake of looking at him like the moment
when everything makes sense. Worse, I've let people
look at me that way. It really is perfect—
Then the head moves, your feet carry you a half step farther.

WHEN I LOOKED TO THE LEAVES

I could only see maps.
Thousands of them. All of their little lines reaching out
from the center, to the edge and over,
and on, and on, and on—

IRRIGATION

That year I dug so many holes that I couldn't
recognize my hands. I shoved rebar
into the ledgy rock of earth with thick fingers.
It was the good life. People smiled at my face.
Fingers touched my arms and stayed. I often
drank until I could not see, and woke to the sun
filling my room like water. Those swimming
mornings I rose and shoveled my feet into boots.

At work the quiet men were afraid to look into my eyes.
In the sweat of a day, my mind rested on dying.
I only wanted to be my father. To be gone
and hanging for someone to find. Always
the furious quaking of leaves on branches returned
me. I poured cement into holes.
The sun would set and end the day. It was nothing,

my job, only a small, daily, world.
With the sun down, over a sink, I ran the hands
at the end of my arms under warm water.
Made sure they were clean, and would not
dirty my dinner as they pulled it apart.
As they placed it in my mouth.

BODIES : BIVOUACS

Scott's brother got hooked on pills after a runaway tire tacoed his truck
at speed on I-25. Scott told me through his new teeth. The old ones

pulled or fallen out from his cigarette-rotten gums.

The porcelain changed the shape of his face. He picked a foil flower
from the ground and said it smelled like heroin. It did.

Awake, we worked in silence. Sometimes I stopped

to bathe my cracked hands in the craven light that seeped from inside.
We dug holes. I laid pipe woven through roots of a mulberry tree. Felt

the weight of the clouds above me like a wet, grey, crown. At home,

young and out of sight, my friends and I would run to a tree that shed
berries like drops of paint onto the silver pavement. We picked

at them desperately, racing the ants, to soak our fingers in the bloodpurple

juice. Pop them over our mouths. Suck our fingers, and wrestling, suck
what was left from the other's. Life was easy then, I think. I've learned

that my memory is only as reliable as breath. In and then out again.

Think of Scott's brother lying in his bed, his body shattered.
His form held together by the cast around him; gauze and glue complete

in the shape of a man. His cast was like a memory. Holding

his body together, the shape of something forgotten. His bones:
a story, begging to be born from the plaster mouth that contained them.

In the sun, shirt stuccoed to my chest, I imagined how it must've felt—

hearing the wind blow through the leaves, creating the world
in each breeze, incapable of turning to see it go by—to be encased.

Immovable. Rebuilt. When we were done, we made sure to replace

the clumps of grass. The mulberry leaves looked veined as hands,
falling onto the turf, pounding it down with our shovel heads. We left

when it looked as if no one would notice we'd been there at all.

GRAY

Years ago, I knew a woman with a wide streak of gray
in her blond hair. She liked to hurt me while we made love.
Called it that. Said, Make love to me. Back then I found it odd,

to think that love could be something created then wielded
in the direction of someone else. She would hit me, sometimes
drew blood. Often burned me with my cigarettes, which she lit

while I lay on my back. I didn't want anything at all. When I saw her
the next morning, she would lift my shirt to my neck and kiss
the bruises and burns where she had left them. I told her once

that I didn't believe I would get old. That something would kill me
first, probably me, whether I meant to or not. We were alone,
in the desert, where the sky opens like a toothless mouth. I rarely

said those things sober, and no, I wasn't sober then. We looked up
at the stars and their silence. Clear out there. She kissed me and said
she would suck the sadness from me, like a snakebite, if I would let her;

then she cut her knuckles on my teeth. That was years ago and I am still
young. I don't know where she is. The last time that I saw her, my nose
was bleeding. There was a half-stubbed cigarette beside us and smoke

in the room. She told me to grab her hair, but only to grab the gray.
She said, Hold me where the color changes, and when I did,
she said, It will all feel like this when we're older.

MARTYRDOM

Getting used to debating angels, I bought bags from Auggie,
out on the corner before he was a saint. Andrew and Matthew
kept clean except for wine, which there was a lot of. Tunics
were dirty. Jesus stayed in his room until he could tie
one on. Catherine would come over with something
to smoke. She had a way about her. Peter was paranoid,
always talking about who was coming and going. Said
one Mary was okay, the other one couldn't come through.
Kept talking about getting out to go fishing. Never left.
Couldn't stand the way Joseph kept checking in on us
making sure we were all fed. Simon wouldn't shut up
bringing little plates and cups, yammering away about
I hope he's all right. I waited till Jesus popped out
to run a saw in the backyard and have a smoke. They
all liked to follow and drag their feet around in the dust.
I had to get out of there, though I should've stayed.
They deserved more, but I had to be saved. John saw me,
tried to hold me down. Thad thought about tying my wrists.
I had to swing a little, Nate caught a couple strays. Philip
thought about trying to stop me, but looked down
at the ground instead. It was a mumbling bunch
for the most part. I threw my shoes on while Judas
practiced tying knots. From the outside, it was just a house,
shingled, shaked, with low sounds coming from
the closed-always windows. Driving by on any given day
you'd have no idea who was inside avoiding the sun.

CATHEDRAL

I have a lie I like to tell myself.
Once, I walked up a hill, fog-crawled,
early spring. Beyond the electric fence
where we kept them, a chicken
in the grass with dew on its feathers.
Its head was gone and so was its blood.
My boots found another, then another,
until I counted seventeen. All headless.
All dry. Vacant. It was a weasel, dug in
beneath the fence. It sucked the blood
and took the heads. We ran a line along
the ground, that snapped electric
when the grass was blown into it
by the wind. I don't claim to know
where the weasel went. I know we lost
some more. Broilers gone to disease,
some drowned looking up in the rain,
though no animal got to them before
we could kill them ourselves.
But that's beside the point.
The point is it wasn't winter, but the trees
were bare, and my mind was filling
in the space where there ought to have
been leaves. There were seventeen bodies
on the ground. It was a mess made not
from lust or anger, but made from something
more than hunger. The weasel wanted
violence and got it. Made it. Then went
to wherever weasels go to sleep it off
while we threw the pale pink carcasses
into a compost pile big enough, hot enough
to turn what they were into mulch.
The weasel slept and wasn't sorry. There's a lie
I like to tell myself: The day came up
and got brighter and brighter.

SPEED

straddle-stood on a moving car dust-lashed
buck-kneed I said *faster* & she kicked
it up a gear • we bought condoms
from the circle k before we went back
I could've fallen but I didn't though
that's really what I wanted • the buick
could haul & the potholes were a trial
& inside she kissed me hard enough
to remind me I could have been anyone
to her • I was drinking then & drunk
& the fast air was cheap • in her room
she put on music that we could
barely hear • it was the lonesome kind
of sex, more body & promises
we knew we couldn't see through
than anything close • when it was her turn
riding on the roof I couldn't bring myself
to get it out of second • she said *faster* & *faster*
& the dust covered the sky enough
that whatever planets & stars & moons
were howling through static • we didn't
speak much after that just let our eyes
& hands work for us • the magnetics
of it electric & polar • I felt it again
last week after a stranger smiled
up at my face & laid her forehead
on my shoulder • It was too kind, too
forgiving of me to bear • the wind
that comes on hot days, working out
on a roof & is so cool & quick it blows
the tension & breath from you
makes every voice silent & closed eyed
& reminds to keep suffering the heat
to feel the breeze again • I still crawl
coward for that • in the morning her room
bloomed shatter nearly green
& I wasn't there to see it

LONG WINTERED

Bonecold, near breaking,
I climbed the cement
stairs to the porch
where I slept.

Working for days, hardly
sleeping. The same
temperature always
inside as out.

Johnny took too much
and lost his mind.
We found him feeling
out the weight

of a kitchen knife
in his hand.
Blade-out-thumb-back.
Said he felt like Jesus.

Said at least like John
the Baptist. Eddie
needed help
working the fiberglass

smooth before
the epoxy went off.
We opened a window
and went back

outside. Left his brother
alone and called
his parents. Said
he's getting religious

again. I don't remember
if it was day
when I turned in.
I know my books

glowed blue though
the light was white.
It was December inside
the house. I stacked

my clothes neatly
where the heat
came up
through the wood

floor. Said
this is me
getting better.
Turns out Johnny's

all right.
Taking it easy.
Before I left
he told me

freedom tastes
like sunlight.
Said I was beat—
the dead leaves,

were getting
to me. They made
a hole
in me where

my matter
had been—
I was a fool to keep
calling it a heart.

NEW HARMONY

There's a rock in the labyrinth and a hole in the rock. You told me that
    you wanted your grief
to be total. You said, like the way love is a board, soaked past its grain
    when the rain falls

and stays. I was thinking about heat. We were staying in a house that creaked.

Behind the walls, the studs didn't meet the beams. When the wind blew
    hard, we could feel
how much whoever had built it had forgotten to do. The roof leaked.
    Rain was pooling

by the bookcase. You said you thought you were losing me. Already
    grieved it. Saw it

through. When the wind blew, the house shook. The house shook when
    the wind blew. I was
thinking about heat. How the hole was made in the rock for water to
    come up through it.

The labyrinth in town was left behind by those who walked it. They did
    it to get closer to god.

We did it to get closer to the middle. You said it was okay if I needed to go.
    I said it wasn't.
There would have been dust, then sludge while someone ran water into
    the bit as it was drilling

to keep it from cracking. Rain was pooling by the bookshelf. At night
    there was no moon.

The road was dark and I was driving with a headlight out. By the bookshelf
    rain was pooling.
We listened to the song silence sings while the car drove through the dark.

It isn't frightening when you ask me to hurt you. It is when you stopped
    having to ask.

Down the road a car was coming with a headlight out: The same one. If
    we were to crash

head on, there would be a moment of perfect symmetry. Listen to the
house shake.

Someone told me once, that I had a black spot on my soul that was never
going to heal.

While we had sex it felt like we were going liquid in each other's arms. At
the center,
in the dark. The water came up through the fountain. Through the fountain,
the water came up.

ROUTINE

Cathedral

I remember my father
teaching me to pray.
I understood the feeling.
Hands pierced with holes.
Head bowed and a crown
that denied resting.
                    The old cathedral
                    tucked into a part
                    of Boston's old city,
                    what they used to call
                    The Combat Zone,
                    where you could never be
safe from sin. He used
to drink there. Snort pills.
Watched his best friend
stabbed to death on the grass.
He loved it there, he said.
                    He would flirt
                    with the drag queens
                    and stand with one leg
                    anchored to a brick wall.
Sober, my father
pointed to the thin
backyard of a brick building.
Explained how a friend
had been drafted
to the war.
                    They got him drunk,
                    right there, a block from the
                    cathedral, took his shoes,
                    lifted his foot onto a stump
                    and placed his empty wallet
                    into his mouth.

His friend did not scream,
only smiled, looking down
at part of himself no longer
belonging to him.

        I think I understood why
        my father could not live
        with us. Inside the stained
        glass he told me to bow
        my head and close my eyes.

He lowered his head.
I lowered mine.
He came to these pews
every day. Twice.
He told me to ask
for the things I wanted.

        I asked for a father. Probably
        for toys.

II.

Routine

I used

        to walk

To keep from drinking.

        Now,

I walk to keep from

        drinking.

Cool air,

        lots of water.

It's hard, even

        when it's easy.

The faucet drips.

        Water lacks

the same way that

        each step

leads

        to another.

There's so much

        I can do.

The moon

        makes a hangnail

mostly.

        Sometimes

a hole, sometimes

        gone.

III.

Engine

My new place is bigger than the last.
There's a backyard, and a deck.
All the more room to fill with wanting—

I was sitting on cobblestones
downtown the first time

someone called me an addict. She was.
I told her, *No*, hot and quick as breath,
though she had seen me:

the powder then my muscles
slacken and braid together again.

I bought Cocoa Puffs from the 7-Eleven
and we shared them sitting on the sidewalk.
She could be dead, relapsed, gone.

Or she could be fine, happy even.
I don't know. I never went back to see her,

though I'd said I would.
Instead, I found rooms with thick curtains
over the windows and got high.

The darkness felt good: the world not knowing
what I was doing. Unable to see.
Later, my friends got worried.

I'd been telling them
I wanted to die, when I'd deleted myself

enough not to remember. In my new place
I sit in its bigness. I only miss using
when I'm alone and convinced

by the myth of my own meaninglessness.
I remember the feeling of being moved

by an engine outside of me.
Silvered and chromed, a piston shooting
not knowing why.

IV.

Routine

Get

high   ripped   wrecked

  ruined   fucked   slammed

sauced   fast   speed   slung   fucked   up

  cracked   out   revved   up   three   sheets

right   stove   in   right   sideways   tuned

up   stove   up   obliderado   deleted

erased   tomorrow   or   the   next

day   wound   winded   wrought   wrung

         sober

I   promise   tripped

      yachted   blown

  crystalled   white   swamped   gone   it   will

never   happen   again   dumb   stupid

sunk   sorry   fucked   dropped   drunk

  crushed   blind   eliminado   freaked   wrong

stumped   stung   drilled   doped

loaded   lit   limed   rung   kicked

what   the   fuck   were   you   thinking

    good

V.

Leaves from the Canopy

My father was a large man. He tried
to be good. I am a large man too,
ordinary otherwise. I'm often sad

and sitting where I can. When I told
my lover how bad I feel she said
maybe I'd had too many French fries

and beers. My father used to say
the hardest part of getting sober
was how much it hurt:

He said you sweat it out and the pores
drip pain. You couldn't do anything
but sit through it, eyes throbbing

with the world a blurred palette
of endlessly mixing colors. He said
The world can get unbearably bright.

The grass here today is simply green.
The leaves, simply greener. I got sober
once. For a while. I lived among trees.

It didn't make me happy. It didn't even hurt.

VI.

Routine

I moved to Maine

lived in a place
where people lived without

I still drove to the bars
every other weekend or so

only had one or two
I met a woman there

thirteen years older than me
we would kiss leaned against my car

cathedral of smoke
when she got off work

we went skinny dipping
it was August and the ocean was alive

small specks of phosphorescent matter
lit up

we could see each other's bodies
toeing the coolness

and the heat
in the water

with the small lights
in the water

I could read
for the first time

the lines across her chest
and she read mine

VII.

Night

I dreamed I was in a plaza full of birds.
They gathered around
a fountain. As I got closer, I saw

there were thin yellow legs standing up
on their own. The birds leapt and pecked
at the legs. Pecked at each other

until there was nothing left.
I've been clean not very long
and the nights wear me. My dreams

betray me. Silver betraying the ore.

VIII.

Routine

We drank beer naked in the river.
He doesn't remember.
Not the way that I do.

How the mountains were brown,
and then grey
and then something darker.

That they opened up.
I mean they moved
while the sun made a show

of its daily resignation.
It was beautiful.
The water was cold.

We wanted to be other people.
And we were while our skin went numb.
It was too vivid, the grass

and the sky wouldn't shut up
while we walked back
to the house.

Thin arms on each other's
waists and the soft wrist
of summer breeze

to take the water away.
It was beautiful. I was happy.
He doesn't remember.

IX.

Katabasis, Down

The real depth was past
the credit card crush
the hard sniff

the head kicked back.
Beyond the open shirts
and sticky skin. My gums

leaving blood
on the pillow
where I laid my head

and tried to sleep.
I've held many bodies
in my arms. I've had my body

held by people who
I hardly knew. They
told me they could taste it

on my breath. This speed:
swift needing. They loved
me anyway, maybe

because of it. The thrill
of being near someone
who has no

control. It was past
the beating heart, the slowing
brain. Thinking I needed

more. It wasn't the thinking
that I would vanish. Sometimes
asking for it. Begging

for it. It was the birdsong
that rose before
the violet dawn and announced

that today had become tomorrow.
The rising. Of shame. Of course
I miss it. Every whistle.

X.

Routine

I stay silent while the sun sets among the bricks
that surround our windowed room. We drink
Pepsi, or coffee, though it's late. Eat Milky Ways,
and attempt to be mindful of them, reminding
our bodies to treat them as if they were the first
consumption. Someone leaves to remove his rage
from the room. We close our eyes and slowly chew.
He rises from his chair, and we feel the breeze
from the open door. The old men are flirting
with the only young woman among us. She is new
too. Neither of us speaks, other than to say our names
and afflictions. The man returns, says he was outside,
watching the cathedral looming in the sky,
and the children who ran home as the streetlights
coming on called in their mother's voices.
We meditate to the sound of a British man,
describing our chakras from a video on YouTube—
their color, location, and access to which
particular parts of our selves we have lost touch.
After, we mill around and smoke cigarettes,
just like everyone describes in their movies and books.
The world is on fire in this light. Orange, and red.
Clouds pink as walls in the drunk tank and the new
woman asks why I've come, away from the men
who chuckle and gesture. I tell her I asked someone
I loved if they loved me back, and to that they said, *yes*
and then *unfortunately.* We agree, while gloaming gives
way to night, that the response had been fair.

XI.

Confession

I do not pray. I never have.

But that's a lie too.

I remind myself to be alive.

I thank myself for my body, thin trap that it is.

Try to be thankful for my chapel of sharp bones.

I only talk to you anymore when I am afraid—

I am in a car and I am suddenly aware that I could never make it home.

Realize that I may join you, or rather that I will.

It would be easy to die like you.

It would be predictable.

LOVE POEM

Before I reached the Crestone Cemetery, I found the fleshless bones of a horse
lying in a weedy ditch. The air was still. It was nearly night. I looked at
   its ribs,

its colossal skull. Dandelions came up through the holes its body made
in the ground. Lamb's ear. Jack-in-the-pulpit. Queen Anne's lace.

Bleeding heart. Someone must have led it there, or it wandered,
but the smooth curtain of its head had been torn by the hot lead of a bullet.

That was certain. I climbed down. It was light enough that I could see
everything. The moon was coming up, over the pines, putting a hole into
   the sky,

a hollow needle pushed through skin. I thought to run my hands over
the smooth bones as if they were wood or stone. I wondered if they could

be touched without flinching. It was just another skeleton that lines the road
like white crosses in that part of America. And yet, the bones seemed to move

as the moonlight moved above them. I moved my finger to where the bullet
had broken, the gaping of eyes. I thought to touch it again, and then, I did.

RESISTANCE

A friend's dog saw me
once, kneeling toward it
and ran, leash dropped,
into traffic. After

the dog was hit, sent flying
and sliding, and after
it stopped and died,
after all that cruel movement,

I walked it off. The horror
on the faces of friends
didn't stop me. I walked
it off. Had a few. Bought

a bag of something fast.
At least one. It's hard
to remember. Those nights
are mostly one

night. In bed, with lamplight
coming from the house
over the yard in right
angles, I can hear cats

screeching in the space
behind me. Screaming
maybe from joy
or pain. It's hard to tell

not seeing them. I'm thinking
about dying again, hearing
them maybe killing
each other outside. I used

to think of it every day.
For a long time. I had
lovers and friends. Now
my mind is like a lake

carved out and empty.
I could go out and check.
Hard telling, not knowing.
But instead I'm inside

looking at the fingerbone
branches of winter reach
up degloved. My aunt
used to tell me not to be

sad. She said her son
was in a better place.
My father too. And another
cousin. All gone

on their own. I haven't
had a sip or a sniff
for the longest time.
She meant it too. Looked

me down hard
and hugged me. Tonight
my mind is a picture
of a lake, dried out with

glass bottles
where the water
ought to be. A friend
explained how he told

his boss he had leukemia
to get time off for rehab.
Not a bad lie, I think.
We both used to get high

on something like *now*.
Or at least that's how
it started. The morning
fills in

what the night took
away. I used to know how

easily I could lose it all.
I could go in the morning

and check. I'll walk out
like I used to and light
a cigarette. One dead cat,
or two. Or

none. The drink got
cheaper the longer
the drinking got. It's
wrong to miss my lover

falling asleep with her hand
around my throat. Fingertips
where the blood pumped
to make sure my heart

wouldn't stop overnight.
Her fear. Her tenderness.
Both waiting
for catastrophe. The sound

is gone, or has been
drowned in the darkness.
I could go check
in the morning, but I won't.

WHY THE TREES

I hadn't realized I relapsed
until I was hugging
a stranger in a black shirt.
In the morning

I was sick of myself
and walked with friends
who didn't know. I'd
told them I'd stay

at the party, and I did. Drinking
beers, and asking louder
and louder for key-fulls
of cocaine from a man

I'd just met. He had a gun
on his hip. He laughed hard
when I told him that
I'd never trust myself

to keep a gun in my house.
He poured lines out
onto his phone and asked
for five dollars a hit. I slept

outside on a stoop while
it rained and walked
the miles home with the stars
hidden and hanging

over my head. Panic
mostly. I named the trees
as I walked, and felt
close to washed for a while.

SCRAP

Off Coronation Island, men would lift
their guns. Barrels toward the water, waiting
for sea lions. I watched. Hauled the catch.
Slow and strung out, sleep was kept from me
like a photo in a locket around
someone else's neck. It was cold in July
and August. I had no idea people made it
that way. Back home smokestacks make
for sightseeing and the water is too dirty for fishing.
Just barges and tugs. You can sit on the shore
and watch. I sat with a friend once on the slab stone
that holds the water back. It was daybreak.
Truth is I have no idea how people make it
anywhere. Tin, 89 cents an inch. $2.50 on copper.
Wrecking yard teeming with itching arms.
Cigarette dangling, someone taught me to strip
the rubber off of wires. We coiled the orange
glinting in our hands. He showed me to a shed,
full of two-fifties all tangled up. It's careful work.
There were no clouds on the Mississippi.
Just boats, and trash, someone else with
a shopping cart full of something corrugated
that had come off a house. Me and my friend.
We watched. It was wonderful to sit with her.
I'm home now and I've got 60 days. They don't shoot
sea lions here, just people. People and dogs.
I remember the river, and how the air would sparkle
off the water. You can hear the alligator shear,
its angry music. I hope I can make it alone. Then,
I don't. You can taste the lead on the wind,
almost sweet. Something like chocolate.

TRANSLATION

My home becomes dark. It is small. It clutters
easily. I cleaned it deep today, then I walked
to the Mississippi, and watched the river move.

I lived once in a windowless room
with strangers. We worked together,
and were housed there. I met a woman then,

drinking by a river, on a roiling night. We kissed
and it meant nothing. She spoke only French,
and so, we did not speak.

We were approached by several street cats.
I knelt: small genuflection. I put out my hand.
She kicked one hard in the side

when it neared her shin. I said, *Stop,*
and that was all I said. Later, making love
in her bed, she said *I could never love you*

in a language I understood. In the morning
we were silent. We drank coffee.
I felt her lips on my cheek in the sun.

MENOTOMY ROCKS PARK

There's ice on the water and fog
on the ice. I grew up near this pond.
Used to skate it, play hockey

until it got dark or our moms
called us home. Now, it's night
and I'm older. After I graduated

someone drowned in the water.
I didn't know her. We all knew her
brother. I must've met her. I feel sorry

for her family. Back when it happened,
and tonight, by the water in the fog.
Last time I was home, I drove to a store

and bought six cans of beer. I drank five
in my car and the last sitting by the pond.
I didn't think of her or anyone else—

I thought of myself. I wonder if I was
a better person when I was drinking.
No one told me I would have to consider

that. I wish I would've met her. I think
we would have gotten along. Maybe not.
I know sadness is a thin thread for tying

two people together. The stone is wet with fog,
the same way our faces used to be with sweat
and frost, amazed at our own speed, or the arc

of something we had made fly away
from us, because of us. Last time I was here
I would go home drunk every night

and my mom would have no idea. I don't think so:
She would open her arms and smile
looking right at me. She would tell me

how happy she was that I had come home.
There's ice on the water and it's too thin
to walk out onto. I'd do anything to fix my heart.

I TURN MY HEAD TO FIND THE WORLD

I come to the tree with the twist in its trunk.
Past the hypodermic needle, nestled into cracked pavement
and yellowed grass. The burls, bulging with infection,

make for turning the most beautiful bowls.
Once I watched a woman I loved cut through a small
white oak with an axe and a hacksaw. Felled, I hauled it

through the forest and snow in a T-shirt, steam rising
from my chest. We had learned what it meant to work together.
To burn and warm. I fed pigs each day at dusk

and dawn. Often, I shocked my hand hard on the electric
fence that kept them penned. They would take my pants
and boot laces up into their mouths, pull me to the ground

and chew my cloth and skin. They never left a mark.
I loved them, purely. Welcomed the electric hurt
that came with the ritual. In the mud

with them, darkness coming or going, I wished
the sun would never rise.
I've been happy for years now, still things are tiresome

and I am vague. This isn't how I expected to feel.
The burl, gnarled like knuckles. The rise and fall.

CONTROLLED BURN

We slept in a cabin. Two long pine beams
ran eave to eave. And though I was holding
my love in my arms I thought, against my will,
that the beam above us would have been high
enough for my father to hang himself from.
It would be high enough for me
to hang myself from. I was relieved
by how fiercely I wanted to be alive. We lay
until it was time to eat, and wandered down
to the valley where friends had made dinner.
In the dark blue night, the flames still burned.
Moved closer as we ate. Above us,
through the smoke, the stars burned, resolved
to be seen long after they were gone. I will
never be ashamed of my hopefulness.
It is the bravest thing about me.

THE CLOUDS REMAIN UNMOVING

Outside, the sky's light unfading:
the clouds impossibly still.
I am in love now. I tell her every day.

She holds me tight in response.
She doesn't know if she'll stay. Through the window,
a cemetery. The graves growing stone

while wind peppers the tall grass beside them.
It's quiet. Her breath makes small myths
in the night. There is nothing more I can do.

AVENUE

Last night a bear swam behind me
the length of a river while I rowed a boat.
The internet says it means I'm being haunted
by some part of me that is untamed. A raw part

nagging the rest of me. In the dream,
there was no fear. On land I could do anything I wanted.
I drank, and dipped my cigarettes into drugs.
In the dream, I knew I was dreaming

and still, I lied to everyone. That old magic trick:
I thought for years my mom didn't know that I drank.
On the phone yesterday, she said it always seemed
that I got drunk just to make myself sad. *You just wanted*

to get to the sad part. She called it an avenue.
She told me she dropped a garbage can full of ice
on her foot. Broke three toes. That a storm
was blowing in. I couldn't believe she knew. I couldn't

believe no one would be there to shovel. I should've
thanked her for letting me think I got away with it. Or,
apologized for being angry at her for years, for
being someone who would miss me if I decided

to disappear. She woke this morning to twenty inches
of snow and a postoperative shoe. I woke this morning
tasting my clumsy sleight of hand. My mouth
was open and my gums were weeping something awful.

TENDER

I was taught that it was pain that makes the body worthy.
Or at least that's what I learned.
I've got scars and ink etched into my skin,
as if those markings somehow make it more alive.
It's been five years since I held my arm on a table,
while two hands pushed into it, the small
circle burning, while I believed the smell
meant something. It meant nothing
other than some sort of letting go. I see it now,
and smile. Quick and shy.
These days, the birdsong wakes me, pushed through
two sets of lungs, unbelievably small.
The dogwoods are blooming.
I used to hate this body.
But it wasn't long ago that someone pushed her thumb
into my mouth to feel my tongue against it. It felt
good. Tender. A small sacrament that wouldn't be swallowed.
In the night last week, I heard an owl call out its question.
First, I thought it was her, then I realized it couldn't be.
That's the kind of suffering I'd like to hold on to now.

THROUGH THE GLASS DARKLY

When I told you what my father did to himself,
you didn't say *sorry*. That was all right, good even.

We made love instead and while I made the skin
against your ribs go taut, you closed your eyes.

The only time I feel the muscles in my shoulders
go slack anymore. You fingered the dark spot

on my hip. Said some people believe birthmarks
show how you died in a past life. The smattering

of small dots on your back like buckshot. Men
were lying prone on the lawn drinking water

and putting food into their mouths. They could
only guess what we were doing inside, probably didn't.

Something tender in the way we tear each other apart.
There's a part of myself that I'm trying to understand.

Maybe it's simple. Most things are. My father
wanted to die, and so he did. We both want risk,

and then oblivion. We give it to each other and watch
through the mirror hung across a doorframe

in the other room. I ran the sulfur out of the faucet
before filling you your glass. The morning sky here

so open it's like an ocean hanging inches from your face.
When we showed each other the things we'd done

to ourselves we laid silent. I'm starting to get it.
Most days they're just facts, and sometimes facts

are only sad and true. We've left each other under
so many skies now. You touched the scar in my face

and then my hip again. Said the spot looked like
an entire continent, or maybe the state of Tennessee.

TO MY FATHER, WHO BELIEVED

You moved my bed into my mother's house while I fed Fritos to Alex the Dog.

I'm 26 this year: a fact.

Scrapyard backyard, we kicked rust around, you drank a beer.

We had a dream the same night that you got sober, and then you did.

Our insides wet. Our insides wet.

We used to go to church but you couldn't take the blood, could only take the body.

Host of pain, glory of his violence, glory of another way—

You took it twice while the priest nodded and knew.

Memories are tamboured, pulled over what happened after, make a hollow sound like skin.

I lived.

They cut the electricity while you sipped soda and your girlfriend danced with me in the cool dark of that one room Boston shack.

When you started telling me that God was in the trees, you were drinking the blood again.

At the funeral, people held pictures of you up beside my face and sobbed at the semblance.

Some are louvered, seen through shutters, clipped, unfinished memories that believe they are real.

I smoked so many cigarettes some nights that my gums bled onto my pillow.

I could double my years: a possibility

Memory is only a rehearsal of oak, endless pain, quiet fields.

I wanted to die to know how you felt, then I grew a beard so I wouldn't see your mirrored face.

It took me so long to see that you could just be dead, not omnipresent.

Dad, I wish you could hear the wind in the leaves again, it sounds just
   the same.

I'll have outlived you: an impossibility.

You said, God was in the corn and the corn was all over the earth.

I haven't got God, but I'm looking for something else.

I keep one photo of us up, neither of us smiling, your face like stone,

mine bright like mine.

AROUND THE SUN

I've got a year sober—
still I'm seeing things.
Stars where stars
shouldn't be.

On an island
with my mother in June.
We walked, swam,
cooked. I snuck out

for cigarettes. Fresh air.
More honest than ever.
I even took a shot at God:
The only holy house

on the island, beside
a lake the color of burlap,
getting lighter and lighter.
When I went in,

I didn't kneel. The priest
took my shoulders
in his hands. Smiled,
gin and cologne. Called

me son. He didn't see
the stars anyway,
little constellations
all over the earth.

Later I showed up
at the bottle return
with a sedan-full
of aluminum and glass.

Got in line to be redeemed
a nickel at a time. Home,
my mother asked
how many cans

there were after all.
She didn't deserve
to have an addict
for a husband,

for a son. I gave her
thirteen dollars
and sixty-five cents.
My anger, senseless,

cruel. I said,
you do the math.
There were no fish
in the lake

when my father died,
drunk and high.
Mom kept saying,
god dammit,

what a waste.
There were only
stars on the water,
stars from the sky.

NOTES

The sentence "I try to keep busy" draws inspiration from a similar line in Mary Jo Bang's "The Circus Watcher."

"Bodies : Bivouacs," draws part of its title and inspiration from the song "Bivouac" by Jawbreaker.

"To My Father, Who Believed" was generated from a writing prompt inspired by the poem "A Horse Named Never," by Jennifer Chang.

In "I Turn My Head to Find the World," the words "things are tiresome and I am vague" were spoken to me by my mother. This is one of endless examples of her disproving her own belief that she "doesn't understand poetry."

ACKNOWLEDGMENTS

To my mother, Amy, thank you for being the strongest person I've known, for raising me on your own, and for never being anything other than loving, supportive, and brave. You deserve the world from me. I hope these poems are enough for now. I love you, Ma, without condition.

Thank you to my father, who loved me fiercely and who I have continued to love since his death, sometimes dangerously. I wish you could have seen these poems.

I cannot express my gratitude and luck to have called such incredible writers my peers over the years. Thank you to Joe Jang, Edil Hassan, Kieron Walquist, Stefania Gomez, Joe Gutierrez, mace dent johnson, Precious Musa, Sanam Sheriff, Asha Futterman, Carlota Gamboa, Abby Frederick, Katy Hargett-Hsu, Safwan Khatib, Gabe Fine, Hollis Schmidt, David Andrews, Paul Ukrainets, Rachel Mannheimer, Noah Baldino, Jim Whiteside, Mark Spero, Rachel Dillon, Sara Cunningham, Aishwarya Sahi, Catherine Liu, Kimberly Cervantes, Stacy Nigliazzo, Anthony Sutton, and Bevin O'Connor. And, of course, Mathew Weitman, who has looked through this manuscript more than anyone and has been so generous and helpful with his time and care. Thank you to everyone who I may have, and certainly have, forgotten to include in this list.

Thank you to Mary Helen Callier for editing advice and much, much more.

Thank you to Maxwell and Rowan Shaw-Jones and Libby Quinn for their love, care, and support throughout my writing and life. I love you.

Thank you to Emily Villano for all of your care your untold impact on and editing of these poems.

Thank you to Mat Dolan, for looking after me, for everything.

Brandon Cobean, my brother, thank you.

Thank you, Melissa Cundieff, for our conversations, for your poems, and for your mind.

Thank you to Carl Phillips for being an incredible mentor both in and out of the classroom. This book would not exist without you.

Thank you, Mary Jo Bang, for your invaluable mentorship as a writer and teacher.

Thank you to Cass Donish for giving me active space and support to explore grief on the page.

Niki Herd, thank you for your support, kindness, and insight.

Nick Flynn, thank you for your ongoing care and support.

francine harris, thank you for our conversations about poetry and music alike.

Thank you to Kevin Prufer, Martha Serpas, Mark Bibbins, Eduardo C. Corral, Roger Reeves, and Mark Wunderlich for your mentorship as well.

Thank you to all of my friends and family outside of the writing world who, gratefully, are too many to list here. I love you all, and I'm so lucky to know you.

Thank you to the creative writing departments of both Washington University in St. Louis and the University of Houston for the support and opportunity during my MFA and PhD. To all my professors and mentors, thank you for your thoughts and guidance in looking over many of the poems in this book.

Thank you to the writing faculty of Colorado College, particularly Felicia Chavez, Olivia Wall, and Di Seuss. A special thanks to Jane Hilberry for being my first teacher of poetry and encouraging me to pursue it as a craft: you allowed me to fall in love with poetry and begin to find my voice. For that, I cannot express my gratitude.

Thank you to the editors and staff of the Poetry Foundation, the Academy of American Poets, and the *Missouri Review*, the *Adroit Journal*, *New Letters* magazine, and the Breadloaf Writers' Conference for support and acknowledgment in the way of awards and selections.

Thank you to Gregory Fraser for selecting my manuscript to be published into this book, and to John Poch, Amy Maddox, and all those involved in the Vassar Miller Prize and the University of North Texas Press.

Thank you to the editors and staff of each journal that has published my work. Some of the poems in this book have been published, or are forthcoming, in the following publications:

POETRY:

Sparks in the Sun

Missouri Review:

Felling
His Body Cut Through the World Like a Cold Wind
Supper Poem
Love Poem

Birmingham Poetry Review:

Kill Switch
Ruby Throat
Avenue
Bodies : Bivouacs
Menotomy Rocks Park

Yale Review:

Inheritance

Permafrost Magazine:

Stillborn

Academy of American Poets, Poets.org:

Irrigation
Cathedral

32 Poems:

Translation
Gray

The Adroit Journal:

Through the Glass Darkly
Around the Sun

Thank you to everyone who I have met through my recovery and has helped keep me sober and living toward the life I have today. You've given me the world when I thought it was gone.

Finally, thank you to anyone and everyone who's taken the time to read my poems and my book. It's an honor I feel all the way through.

Kelan Nee

Printed in the USA
CPSIA information can be obtained
at www.ICGtesting.com
JSHW081146190524
63083JS00005B/20

9 781574 419313